Power Privilege and Justice:
Private Prison for Profit

.MR. Robert K Boscarato

.

ISBN-13:
978-1497597136

ISBN-10:
1497597137

DEDICATION

Insert dedication text here. Insert dedication text here. Insert dedication text here. Insert dedication text here. Insert dedication text here. Insert dedication text here. Insert dedication text here. Insert dedication text here. Insert dedication text here. Insert dedication text here.

Power Privilege and Justice

Power Privilege and Justice

Power Privilege and Justice

ACKNOWLEDGMENTS

Insert acknowledgments text here. Insert acknowledgments text here. Insert acknowledgments text here. Insert acknowledgments text here. Insert acknowledgments text here. Insert acknowledgments text here. Insert acknowledgments text here. Insert acknowledgments text here. Insert acknowledgments text here. Insert acknowledgments text here.

Contents

Private prisons in the United Kingdom

Development

In the modern era, the United Kingdom was the first country in all of Europe to use prisons run by the private sector to hold its prisoners. Wolds Prison opened as the first privately managed prison in the UK in 1992.,[1] as one of a number of prisons built by the public sector but contracted to the private sector to

Private prison

.A **private prison** or **for-profit prison**, **jail**, or **detention center** is a place in which individuals are physically confined or interned by a third party that is contracted by a government agency. Private prison companies typically enter into contractual agreements with governments that commit prisoners and then pay a per diem or monthly rate for each prisoner confined in the facility.

Today, the privatization of prisons refers both to the takeover of existing public facilities by private operators and to the building and operation of new and additional prisons by for-profit prison companies.

operate under 5 year contracts. Soon private prisons were established under the government's Private Finance Initiative, where contracts are awarded for the entire design, construction, management and finance of a prison under 25 year contracts. Later, Government attempted to 'market test' prisons operated by the public sector, though no prison transferred from public to private operation through this route until Birmingham in 2011.[2] Prisons operated by the private sector are subject to re-competition at the end of the contract, when the public sector may bid, and on 3 occasions has done so successfully.

Privately run prisons are run under contracts which set out the standards that must be met. Payments may be deducted for poor performance against the contract. Government monitors ('controllers') work permanently within each privately managed prison to check on conditions and treatment of prisoners, and privately run prisons are subject to inspection by HM Chief Inspector of Prisons in the same way as publicly run ones. There are now 14 prisons in England and Wales operated under contract by private companies. Between them they have the capacity to hold about 13,500 prisoners or approximately 15% of the entire prison population. There are also 2 privately run prisons in Scotland. Current operators in the United Kingdom are G4S (6), Sodexo Justice Services (formerly known as

Kalyx, and prior to that UKDS) (4) and Serco (6).

A competition is in progress to run 9 prisons in England and Wales. The first stage of the results was announced on 8 November 2012: the public sector will retain 3 and also take over Wolds Prison, currently run by G4S. The other 5 prisons will be subject of further competition between Serco, Sodexo and a new company, MTC/Amey.[3] At the same time, Ministers outlined plans to contract out all but core custodial functions at all public sector prisons with the aim of saving £450m over 6 years. The loss of G4S of Wolds Prison and its failure to win any new contracts was widely linked to the company's failures with its contract for the 2012 Olympics.

HM Prison Ashfield opened in 1999 and was the first private prison in the UK to house young offenders. The prison was soon mired in controversy after repeated riots and reports of poor management. Conditions at the prison became so bad in 2003 that the Youth Justice Board withdrew prisoners from Ashfield, and threatened to recommend that the prison should be taken over by the public sector.[4] Conditions at the prison improved however and the jail remained privately managed. Buckley Hall Prison was originally opened as a privately managed prison in 1994, but after a competitive tendering process in 2000, management of the prison was transferred to Her Majesty's Prison Service[5]

Private prisons in the United States
Early history

The privatization movement can be traced to the contracting out of confinement and care of prisoners after the American Revolution. Deprived of the ability to ship criminals and undesirables to the Colonies, Great Britain began placing them on <u>hulks</u> (used as <u>prison ships</u>) moored in English ports.[6]

The partial transfer of San Quentin prison administration from private to public did not mark the end of privatization. The next phase began with the <u>Reconstruction Period</u> (1865–1876) in the south, after the end of the Civil War. Plantations and businessmen needed to find replacements for the labor force once their slaves had been freed. Beginning in 1868, <u>convict leases</u> were issued to private parties to supplement their workforce.[7][8] This system remained in place until the early 20th century.

Development

Federal and state government has a long history of contracting out specific services to private firms, including medical services, food preparation, vocational training, and inmate transportation. The 1980s, though, ushered in a new era of prison privatization. With a burgeoning prison population resulting from the <u>War on Drugs</u> and increased use of incarceration, prison overcrowding and rising costs became increasingly problematic for local, state, and federal governments.

In response to this expanding criminal justice system, private business interests saw an opportunity for expansion, and consequently, private-sector involvement in prisons moved from the simple contracting of services to contracting for the complete management and operation of entire prisons.[9]

The modern private prison business first emerged and established itself publicly in 1984 when the Corrections Corporation of America (CCA) was awarded a contract to take over a facility in Hamilton County, Tennessee. This marked the first time that any government in the country had contracted out the complete operation of a jail to a private operator.[10] The following year, CCA gained further public attention when it offered to take over the entire state prison system of Tennessee for $200 million. The bid was ultimately defeated due to strong opposition from public employees and the skepticism of the state legislature.[11] Despite that initial defeat, CCA since then has successfully expanded, as have other for-profit prison companies. As of December 2000, there were 153 private correctional facilities (prisons, jails and detention centers) operating in the United States with a capacity of over 119,000.[12] In the past two decades CCA has seen its profits increase by more than 500 percent.[13]

The trend toward privately operated correctional facilities has continued with 85,604 adults (3.7% of the total

US prison population) now housed in 107 privately operated prisons as of 2011[14] Companies operating such facilities include the <u>Corrections Corporation of America</u>, the <u>GEO Group</u>, Inc. (formerly known as Wackenhut Securities), and <u>Community Education Centers</u>. Corrections Corporation of America (CCA) has a capacity of more than 80,000 beds in 65 correctional facilities. The GEO Group operates 57 facilities with a capacity of 49,000 offender beds.[15] The company owns or runs more than 100 properties that operate more than 73,000 beds in sites across the world.[16]

Most privately run facilities are located in the southern and western portions of the United States and include both state and federal offenders.[14] For example, <u>Pecos, Texas</u> is the site of the largest private prison in the world, the <u>Reeves County Detention Complex</u>, operated by the GEO Group.[17] It has a capacity of 3,763 prisoners in its three sub-complexes,[18]

Cost/Benefit analysis

Studies, some partially industry-funded, often conclude that states can save money by using for-profit prisons. However, academic or state-funded studies have found that private prisons tend to keep more low-cost inmates and send others back to state-run prisons.[19] Others[who?] have contended that ostensible cost savings come at the expense of security, and considerable costs are externalized.

In the wake of the <u>escape of three murderers</u> from the minimum/medium security <u>Kingman Prison</u>, <u>Arizona</u> operated by <u>Management and Training Corporation</u> (MTC), and its gruesome aftermath, Arizona Attorney General and gubernatorial candidate <u>Terry Goddard</u> said "I believe a big part of our problem is that the very violent inmates, like the three that escaped, ended up getting reclassified [as a lower risk] quickly and sent to private prisons that were just not up to the job."[20] The private prison had inadequate patrols and prisoner movement, excessive false alarms, a lax culture, and inconsistencies in visitor screening procedures.[21] One escaping murderer, Daniel

Renwick, immediately absconded with the intended getaway vehicle, abandoning his companions outside the prison. He was involved in a shootout in Rifle, Colorado, about 30 hours after the prison break, and was captured by a Garfield County deputy and Rifle police.[22] Though he still "owed" Arizona 32 years on his sentence, he was sentenced to sixty years to be served first in Colorado.[23]

In the course of evading pursuers, the remaining two escapees and their female accomplice, Casslyn Welch, kidnapped vacationing Oklahomans Gary and Linda Haas in New Mexico. The couple was soon murdered by the ringleader, John McCluskey. The extended family of the murdered couple sued the state of Arizona, as well as Dominion, an <u>Edmond, Oklahoma</u> corporation that spec-built the prison, and MTC, the corporation that managed it, for $40 million.[24][25] The last escapees and their accomplice were soon captured. Tracy Province, a lifer, was apprehended in Wyoming on August 9th. The final pair were arrested on August 19th, 20 days after the jailbreak, upon their return to Arizona. All three were first convicted of the escapes, initial hijacking, kidnappings and robberies in Kingman, Arizona. Then they were charged with the same crimes plus murder in New Mexico. John McCluskey, the ringleader, and his accomplice, Casslyn Welch, were also alleged to have committed an armed robbery in Arkansas.[26] The three were eventually held on federal murder charges in New Mexico. McCluskey was tried on death penalty charges but after five months of court proceedings, his jury gave him life imprisonment on December 11, 2013.

Estimates of the costs of the nationwide searches as well as the apprehensions, prosecutions and subsequent imprisonment in the three states greatly exceed a million dollars.[27]

Costs

Proponents of privately run prisons contend that cost-savings and efficiency of operation place private prisons at an advantage over public prisons and support the argument for privatization, but some research casts doubt on the validity of these arguments, as evidence has shown that private prisons are neither demonstrably more cost-effective, nor more efficient than public prisons.[9] An evaluation of 24 different studies on cost-effectiveness revealed that, at best, results of the question are inconclusive and, at worst, there is no difference in cost-effectiveness.[28]

A study by the U.S. Bureau of Justice Statistics found that the cost-savings promised by private prisons "have simply not materialized."[29] Some research has concluded that for-profit prisons cost more than public prisons.[30] Furthermore, cost estimates from privatization advocates may be misleading, because private facilities often refuse to accept inmates that cost the most to house.

A 2001 study concluded that a pattern of sending less expensive inmates to privately run facilities artificially inflated cost savings.[31] A 2005 study found that Arizona's public facilities were seven times more likely to house violent offenders and three times more likely to house those convicted of more serious offenses.[32] A 2011 report by the American Civil Liberties Union point out that private prisons are more costly, more violent and less accountable than public prisons, and are actually a major contributor to increased mass incarceration.[33] This is most apparent in Louisiana, which has the highest incarceration rate in the world and houses the majority of its inmates in for-profit facilities.[34] A 2014 study by a doctoral candidate at UC Berkeley shows that minorities make up a greater percentage of inmates at private prisons than in their public counterparts, largely because minorities are cheaper to incarcerate. According to the study, for-profit prison operators, in particular CCA and GEO Group, accumulate these low-cost inmates "through explicit and implicit exemptions written into contracts between these private prison management companies and state departments of correction."[35]

Staff training

Evidence suggests that lower staff levels and training at private facilities may lead to increases in incidences of violence and escapes. A nationwide study found that assaults on guards by inmates were 49 percent more frequent in private prisons than in government-run prisons. The same study revealed that assaults on fellow inmates were 65 percent more frequent in private prisons.[36]

Lobbying

The influence of the for-profit prison industry on the government has been described as the Prison–industrial complex.[37][38][39]

CCA and The GEO Group have been members the American Legislative Exchange Council (ALEC), a Washington, D.C. based public policy organization that develops model legislation that advances free-market principles such as privatization. Under their Criminal

Justice Task Force, ALEC has developed model bills which State legislators can then consult when proposing "<u>tough on crime</u>" initiatives including "<u>Truth in Sentencing</u>" and "<u>Three Strikes" laws</u>. By funding and participating in ALEC's Criminal Justice Task Forces, critics argue, private prison companies influence legislation for tougher, longer sentences.[40] Writing in *Governing* magazine in 2003, Alan Greenblatt states:

" ALEC has been a major force behind both privatizing state prison space and keeping prisons filled. It put forward bills providing for mandatory minimum sentences and three-strikes sentencing requirements. "

About 40 states passed versions of ALEC's Truth in Sentencing model bill, which requires prisoners convicted of violent crimes to serve most of their sentences without chance of parole.[41]

According to a 2010 report by *NPR*, ALEC arranged meetings between the Corrections Corporation of America and Arizona's state legislators such as Russell Pearce at the Grand Hyatt in Washington, D.C. to write Arizona SB 1070, which would keep CCA's immigrant detention centers stuffed with detainees.[42][43]

CCA and GEO have both engaged in state initiatives to increase sentences for offenders and to create new crimes, including, CCA helping to finance <u>Proposition 6</u> in California in 2008 and GEO lobbying for <u>Jessica's Law</u>[44] in Kansas in 2006. In 2012, The CCA sent a letter to 48 states offering to buy public prisons in exchange for a promise to keep the prisons at 90% occupancy for 20 years.[45][46] States that sign such contracts with prison companies must reimburse them for beds that go unused; in 2011, Arizona agreed to pay <u>Management & Training Corporation</u> $3 million for empty beds when a 97 percent quota wasn't met.[47]

Judicial Corruption Scandal

In the <u>Kids for cash scandal</u>, Mid-Atlantic Youth Services Corp, a private prison company which runs juvenile facilities, was found guilty of paying two judges, <u>Mark Ciavarella</u> and <u>Michael Conahan</u>, $2.6m to send 2000 children to their prisons for such crimes as trespassing in vacant buildings and stealing DVDs from Wal-Mart.[48][49]

Opposition

Many organizations have called for a moratorium on construction of private prisons, or for their outright abolition.[50] The religious denominations <u>Presbyterian Church (U.S.A.)</u> and <u>United Methodist Church</u> have also joined the call, as well as the Catholic Bishops of the South organization.[51]

As of 2013, there has been a modest pushback against the private prison industry, with protests forcing GEO Group to withdraw its $6 million offer for naming rights of <u>FAU</u>

Stadium, and Kentucky allowing its contract with the CCA to expire, ending three decades of allowing for-profit companies to operate prisons in that state.[52] In 2014, Idaho will be taking over the operation of the Idaho Correctional Center from the CCA, which has been the subject of a plethora of lawsuits alleging rampant violence, understaffing, gang activity and contract fraud. Idaho governor Butch Otter, a champion of privatization, said "In recognition of what's happened, what's happening, it's necessary. It's the right thing to do. It's disappointing because I am a champion of privatization."[53]

Attempts to limit privatization and increase oversight

Some U.S. states have imposed bans,

population limits, and strict operational guidelines on private prisons:

- **Banning privatization of state and local facilities**—<u>Illinois</u> in 1990 (Private Correctional Facility Moratorium Act), and <u>New York</u> in 2000, enacted laws that ban the privatization of prisons, correctional facilities and any services related to their operation. <u>Louisiana</u> enacted a moratorium on private prisons in 2001.

- **Banning speculative private prison construction**—For-profit prison companies have built new prisons before they were awarded privatization contracts in order to lure state contract approval. In 2001,

Wisconsin's joint budget committee recommended language to ban all future speculative prison construction in the state. Such anticipatory building dates back to at least 1997, when <u>Corrections Corporation of America</u> built a 2,000-bed facility in <u>California</u> at a cost of $80–100 million with no contract from the <u>California Department of Corrections</u>; a CCA official was quoted as saying, "<u>If we build it, they will come</u>".[54]

. **Banning exportation and importation of prisoners**—To ensure that the state retains control over the quality and security of correctional facilities,

<u>North Dakota</u> passed a bill in 2001 that banned the export of Class A and AA felons outside the state. Similarly, <u>Oregon</u> allowed an existing exportation law to sunset in 2001, effectively banning the export of prisoners. Several states have considered banning the importation of prisoners to private facilities.

• **Requiring standards comparable to state prisons—** <u>New Mexico</u> enacted legislation that transfers supervision of private prisons to the state Secretary of Corrections, ensuring that private prisons meet the same standards as public facilities. In 2001, <u>Nebraska</u> legislation that requires private prisons to meet public prison standards was overwhelmingly approved by the legislature, but <u>pocket-vetoed</u> by the governor. <u>Oklahoma</u> passed a law in 2005 that requires private prisons to have emergency plans in place and mandates state notification of any safety incidents.

Private prisons in Canada

There have only been two private detention facilities in Canada to date, and both reverted to government control.

The only private prison in Canada was the maximum-security <u>Central North Correctional Centre</u>, <u>Penetanguishene</u>, <u>Ontario</u>, operated by the US-based <u>Management and Training Corporation</u> from its opening in 2001 through the end of its first contract period in 2006. The contract was held by the Ontario provincial Ministry of Community Safety and Correctional Services. A government comparison between the Central North "super-jail" and a nearly identical facility found that the public-run prison had measurably better outcomes.[55]

Additionally the GEO Group built the New Brunswick Miramichi Youth Detention Center under contract with the provincial Department of Public Safety, then had its contract ended in the 1990s after public protests.[56]

As of mid-2012, private prison companies continued to lobby the Correctional Service of Canada for contract business.[57]

Attempt to establish private

prisons in Israel

In 2004, the <u>Israeli</u> <u>Knesset</u> passed a law permitting the establishment of private prisons in Israel. The Israeli government's motivation was to save money by transferring prisoners to facilities managed by a private firm. The state would pay the franchisee $50 per day for each inmate, sparing itself the cost of building new prisons and expanding the staff of the <u>Israel Prison Service</u>. In 2005, the human rights department of the Academic College of Law in <u>Ramat Gan</u> filed a petition to the <u>Israeli Supreme Court</u> challenging the law. The petition relied on two arguments. First, it said, transferring prison powers to private hands would violate the prisoners' fundamental human rights to liberty and dignity. Secondly, a private organization always aims to maximize profit, and would therefore seek to cut costs by, for instance, skimping on prison facilities and paying its guards poorly, thus further undermining the prisoners' rights. As the case awaited decision, the first prison was built by the concessionaire, Lev Leviev's Africa-Israel - a facility near Beersheba planned to accommodate 2,000 prisoners.

In November 2009, an expanded panel of 9 judges of the Israeli Supreme Court ruled that privately run prisons are unconstitutional, finding that for the State to transfer authority for managing the prison to a private contractor whose aim is monetary profit would severely violate the prisoners' basic human rights to dignity and freedom. Supreme Court President <u>Dorit Beinisch</u>, wrote that "Israel's basic legal principles hold that the right to use force in general, and the right to enforce criminal law by putting people behind bars in particular, is one of the most fundamental and one of the most invasive powers in the state's jurisdiction. Thus when the power to incarcerate is transferred to a private corporation whose purpose is making money, the act of depriving a person of [their] liberty loses much of its legitimacy. Because of this loss of legitimacy, the violation of the prisoner's right to liberty goes beyond the violation entailed in the incarceration itself."[58]

Media coverage.
Documentary

- Kids for Cash scandal was featured in *Capitalism: A Love Story*, the 2009 documentary by Michael Moore.
- A full-length documentary covering the Kids for Cash scandal entitled *Kids for Cash* was released in February 2014.[59]

Drama

- Kids for Cash scandal has also led to several portrayals in fictional works. Both the *Law & Order: SVU* episode "Crush" and an episode of *The Good Wife* featured corrupt judges sending children to private detention centers. An episode of *Cold Case* called "Jurisprudence" is loosely based on this event.[60][61][62]

See also

- <u>Correctional Services Corporation</u>
- <u>East Mississippi Correctional Facility</u>
- <u>Prison–industrial complex</u>
- <u>Wackenhut</u> Corp.
- <u>Walnut Grove Correctional Facility</u>

• •

Corrections Corporation of America

From Wikipedia, the free encyclopedia

Jump to: <u>navigation</u>, <u>search</u>

Corrections Corporation of America

Type	Public
Traded as	NYSE: CXW
Industry	Private prisons
Founded	Nashville, TN (1983)
Founder(s)	Tom Beasley T. Don Hutto Doctor (i.e., given first name) Robert Crants
Headquarters	Nashville, TN, USA
Area served	United States
Key people	**John D. Ferguson** Chairman of the Board **Damon T.**

	Hininger President & CEO
Revenue	$ 1.736 billion
Operating income	$ 332.06 million
Net income	$ 162.51 million
Total assets	$ 3.020 billion
Total equity	$ 1.408 billion
Employees	16,750 – December 2011
Website	www.cca.com
References:	2011 financial statements[1]

Eden Detention Center in <u>Eden,</u>
<u>Texas</u>

<u>Tallahatchie County Correctional</u>
<u>Facility</u>

Corrections Corporation of America (**CCA**) is a company that owns and manages <u>private prisons</u> and detention centers and operates others on a concession basis. The company is the largest private corrections company in the United States and manages more than 67 facilities with a designed capacity of 92,500 beds. CCA, incorporated in 1983 by three businessmen with experience in government and corrections, is based in <u>Nashville, Tennessee</u>.[2]

Controversies involving the company include: treatment of inmates and disclosure of oversight, lobbying efforts to conceal details of operations, a lawsuit about gang influence in Idaho prison and substantial falsification of records, co-operation with local law enforcement in a school drug sweep, and the deadly 2012 riot in a Mississippi facility.[3]

Contents

History

Corrections Corporation of America (CCA) was founded on January 28, 1983, by Tom Beasley, Doctor Robert Crants and T. Don Hutto.[4] The first facility, the Houston Processing Center, was opened in 1984 and was contracted by the U.S. Department of Justice for the Bureau of Immigration and Customs Enforcement (formerly Immigration and Naturalization Service). The Houston Detention Center was built to house individuals who are awaiting a decision on their immigration case or repatriation.[5]

In 1984, CCA also took over the operations of the Tall Trees non-secure juvenile facility, for the Juvenile Court of Memphis and

Shelby County. Two years later, CCA built the 200-bed Shelby Training Center in Memphis to house juvenile male-offenders.

In 1989, the New Mexico Women's Correctional Facility was opened in Grants, New Mexico; the facility has 204 beds.[6]

In 1990, CCA opened the first medium-security privately operated prison, Winn Correctional Center, in Winn Parish, Louisiana.[7]

The Leavenworth Detention Center, operated for the U.S. Marshals Service, was opened in 1992, the 256-bed facility was the first maximum-security private prison under direct contract with a federal agency.[8]

The ACLU, which sued on behalf of inmates in 2010, claimed that understaffing contributed to the high levels of violence there.[2] In 2014, the <u>Federal Bureau of Investigation</u> (FBI) began an investigation of the CCA management of the <u>Idaho Correctional Center</u> to ascertain whether any Federal statutes were violated regarding the understaffing of the facility and falsification of staffing records.

Overview[edit]

Founded in 1983, Corrections Corporation of America (CCA) owns or operates jails and prisons on contract with federal, state and local governments. CCA designs, builds, manages and operates correctional facilities and detention centers for the Federal Bureau of Prisons, Immigration and Customs Enforcement, the United States

Marshals Service, as well as facilities across the United States.

CCA houses approximately 90,000 offenders and detainees in its more than 60 facilities and employs more than 17,000 nationwide.

The American Correctional Association (ACA) has accredited 90% of CCA's facilities.[10] ACA's Accreditation is a system of verification that correctional agencies and facilities comply with national standards promulgated by the American Correctional Association. Accreditation is achieved through a series of reviews, evaluations, audits and hearings.[11]

Facilities[edit]

CCA operates more than 60 prisons across the U.S.[12]

The T. Don Hutto Residential

Center, a former medium-security prison in Taylor, Texas, which, from 2006 to 2009, held immigrant detainees ages 2 and up under a pass-through contract with Immigration and Customs Enforcement (ICE) division of Homeland Security.[13]

After local and national protests, federal officials announced on August 6, 2009, that it would no longer house immigrant families.[14] Instead, only female detainees will be housed there. In September 2009, the last families left the facility and were moved to the Berks Family Residential Center in Pennsylvania.[15]

As of June 2013, Kentucky is not renewing its contract with Corrections Corporation of America for the Marion Adjustment Center in

St. Mary, ending three decades of allowing outside companies to incarcerate inmates for the state.[16]

Inmate rehabilitation

A critical aspect of America's prison system includes reentry and rehabilitation programs for inmates.[17] Such programs often include education, vocational training, addiction treatment as well as faith-based programs.

CCA says it offers basic adult education, post-secondary education, GRE preparation and testing and literacy programs to all inmates. The Department of Justice's Bureau of Justice Statistics reported in 2008 that only 60% of privately run facilities offered programming to inmates.

According to national research, providing inmates with education and vocational programs can reduce the likelihood that offenders will commit new offenses upon release and return to prison.[18]

In 1993, CCA launched the LifeLine substance abuse training program at the Metro-Davidson County Detention Facility in Nashville, Tennessee. The program is now available in 23 of CCA's 60 facilities.[19]

In addition to the reentry and rehabilitation programs prisons often offer inmates recreational and optional faith-based opportunities, which is an integral part of inmate rehabilitation[20]

Occupancy and profitability

In a 1990s report, Prudential Securities was bullish on CCA but noted, "It takes time to bring inmate population levels up to where they cover costs. Low occupancy is a drag on profits... company earnings would be strong if CCA succeeded in ramp(ing) up population levels in its new facilities at an acceptable rate".[21] In 2011, responding to an initiative from the State of Ohio to reduce "overhead costs by saving $13 million annually while adding 700 beds to house inmates in the overcrowded system," Corrections Corporation of America agreed to buy the Lake Erie Correctional Institution for $72.7 million. This represents a change of policy for CCA, which previously always constructed their own prisons, and was contingent on the Ohio Department of Rehabilitation and Correction agreeing to contractual occupancy requirements [3]. The failure to find a buyer for many other prisons the State offered for sale was taken as good news by the Ohio Civil Service Employees Association, the union for prison guards.

In 2012, CCA sent a letter to prison officials in 48 states, offering to buy prisons from these states in exchange for a 20-year management contract and a guaranteed occupancy rate of 90%.[22] Community organizations have criticized the proposals, arguing that the contractual obligations of states to fill the prisons to 90% occupancy are poor public policy that could force communities into creating criminals, and that these contractual clauses end up costing taxpayers more than state-run prisons would.[23]

Recognition

CCA was named in 2008 as one of the 100 best corporate citizens by Corporate Responsibility Officer magazine.[24] The national military magazine GI Jobs has highlighted CCA as a solid employer for veterans[25] and also named CCA as one of its "Top 50 Military Friendly Jobs" on four[*not in citation given*] separate occasions.[26]

Controversies

Treatment of inmates and disclosure of shortcomings of oversight

Responding to an inmate's death in 2006 at CCA's immigration jail in Eloy, Arizona, government investigators found the medical care provided meant that "detainee welfare is in jeopardy". A subsequent inmate death at the facility resulted in an additional inquiry and "another scathing report," according to the *New York Times*.[27]

Lack of disclosure from government officials charged with overseeing the care provided resulted in an August 2009 ACLU lawsuit. This resulted in disclosure by the Obama administration that 1 in 10 deaths among inmates in immigration detention facilities had been omitted from a list of deaths presented to Congress earlier that year. Two of those deaths took place at CCA's Eloy Detention Center.[28] CCA's Eloy jail had nine known fatalities – more than any other immigration jail under contract to the federal government according to documents obtained in 2009 under FOIA requests by the *New York Times* and the ACLU.[28]

In 2013, CCA confirmed that an internal review showed the corporation falsified records involving about 4,800 employee hours over a period of seven months in the Idaho state prison it operated.[29] In 2014 a subsequent KPMG audit showed the actual overbilling was for over 26,000 hours. Governor Butch Otter ordered Idaho State Police to investigate to see if criminal charges should be brought. Otter had received a total of $20,000 in campaign contributions from employees of the company since 2003. [30] In March, it was announced that the FBI had stepped in to take over the investigation, one that extended to CCA operations in other states.[31]

In the fall of 2012, state auditors of the Lake Erie Correctional Institution in Ohio, acquired by the CCA in January of the same year, deducted $500,000 for contract violations and inadequate staffing.[32]

Lobbying efforts

CCA lobbyists have worked to pass or defeat private prison legislation in many localities, including Texas, New York, Illinois and Tennessee.[33] CCA spent $17.4 million lobbying the Department of Homeland Security, U.S. Immigrations and Customs Enforcement (ICE), the Office of Management and Budget, the Bureau of Prisons, both houses of Congress, and others between 2002 and 2012; including $1.9 million in campaign contributions.[34][35]

According to the *Boston Phoenix*, CCA spent more than $2.7 million from 2006 through September 2008 on lobbying for stricter laws.[36] CCA responded that it does not lobby lawmakers to increase jail time or push for longer sentences under any circumstance, noting that it "educates officials on the benefits of public-private partnership but does not lobby on crime and sentencing policies."[34] Among its risk factors listed in its 10-K annual report as required by the SEC, CCA includes the following:

"The demand for our facilities and services could be adversely affected by the relaxation of enforcement efforts, leniency in conviction or parole standards and sentencing practices or through the decriminalization of certain activities that are currently proscribed by our criminal laws. For instance, any changes with respect to drugs and controlled substances or illegal immigration could affect the number of persons arrested, convicted, and sentenced, thereby potentially reducing demand for correctional facilities to house them."[23]

At the federal level, the corporation's lobbying focuses largely on immigrant detention. In 2012, CCA spent $1,790,000 lobbying Congress and federal bureaucracies on issues relating to homeland security, law enforcement, immigrant detention,

and information disclosure
legislation.[37]

Lawsuit about gang influence in Idaho prison

In 2010 the corporation was being
investigated by the FBI for an
incident at their prison in Idaho
Correctional Center. A video released
by the Associated Press showed a
prison inmate being beaten
unconscious with guards watching
not taking action. Because the matter
was then under litigation, the
company had only said publicly that
the release of the video is "an
unnecessary security risk to our staff,
the inmates entrusted to our care and
ultimately to the public." CCA said it
was cooperating with investigators.[38]
In March 2010, The ACLU filed suit
against CCA in Idaho alleging that

guards were not protecting inmates from other violent inmates.[39] In February 2014, the federal judge hearing the case awarded $349,000 to the ACLU for its costs in bringing the action.[40]

In November 2012, eight inmates filed a federal lawsuit in Idaho alleging that CCA prison officials partially ceded control of the Idaho Correctional Center to gang leaders. The lawsuit cited Idaho Department of Correction reports suggesting that the Aryan Knights and the Severely Violent Criminals were able to wrest control from staff members after prison officials began housing members of the same gangs together in some cell blocks to reduce violent clashes.[41][42] In September 2013, a federal judge held CCA in <u>contempt of court</u> for persistently understaffing the Idaho Correctional Center in direct violation of a legal settlement.[43] In October 2013, CCA was encouraged not to bid on a new contract to continuing running the Idaho Correctional Center. The state will reassume control of its prison on July 1, 2014.[44]

Co-operation with local law enforcement in a school drug sweep

In 2012, CCA conducted a drug sweep of <u>Vista Grande High School</u> in <u>Casa Grande, Arizona</u> in concert with local law enforcement. The program director of the Tucson office of the <u>American Friends Service Committee</u> said "It is chilling to think that any school official would be willing to put vulnerable students at risk this way."[45]

2012 riot in Mississippi facility

In May 2012 a riot at CCA-operated Adams County Correctional Facility in Natchez, Mississippi claimed the life of a Corrections Officer and left sixteen staff members and three prisoners injured. Twenty-five employees were held hostage during the disturbance which was ultimately quelled by facility staff with assistance from the Mississippi Highway Patrol and the Federal Bureau of Prisons.[46]

According to a company statement, the fatality was the second time an employee had "lost his life to inmate assault."[47]

The riot came on the heels of the unexplained death of an inmate at

CCA's <u>Reeves County Detention Complex</u>, who had suffered several epileptic seizures in the facility in preceding months, and had been denied a change in medication to one prescribed to him previous to his detention, which he stated had been successful at controlling the seizures.[48]

• •
• •

Christina Crain Unit
From Wikipedia, the free encyclopedia
Jump to: <u>navigation</u>, <u>search</u>
Christina Melton Crain Unit

Location	1401 State School Road Gatesville, Texas 76599-2999
Coordinates	◆31°28'17"N 97°44'26"W31.4713889°N 097.7405556°W
Status	Operational
Security class	G1-G4, Transient, Outside Trusty, Developmentally Disabled, Substance Abuse
Capacity	Unit: 1,498; Boot Camp: 8 SAFP: 288; Trusty Camp: 321
Opened	August 1980
Former name	Gatesville Unit
Managed by	TDCJ Correctional Institutions Division

Warden	Lorretta Carmona
County	Coryell County
Country	USA
Telephone	+1 254 865 8431
Website	www.tdcj.state.tx.us/unit_directory../gv.html

The **Christina Melton Crain Unit** (formerly the **Gatesville Unit**) is a Texas Department of Criminal Justice prison for females in Gatesville, Texas. The prison is along Texas State Highway 36, 3 miles (4.8 km) north of central Gatesville. The unit, with about 1,317 square feet (122.4 m^2) of space, is co-located with the Hilltop Unit, the Dr. Lane Murray Unit, and the Linda Woodman Unit.[1] The unit's regular program houses around 1,500 women, and it is one of Texas's main prisons for women.[2] Female prison offenders of the TDCJ are released from this unit.[3] With a capacity of 2,013 inmates, Crain is the TDCJ's largest female prison.[4]

Contents

[hide]

History

Topographical map of the Gatesville prison units (Crain, Mountain View, Hilltop, and Hughes), U.S. Geological Survey, 1994

The Gatesville Unit, formed on portions of the former Gatesville State School,[5] opened in August 1980.[1] The portions of Gatesville State School that became the Crain Unit include the Live Oak,[6] Riverside,[7] Sycamore,[8] Terrace, and Valley schools, while the Hackberry and Hilltop units of the former state school became the Hilltop Unit.[7] The Gatesville Unit was named after the City of Gatesville.[9]

From its opening until several years before 2010, the Gatesville Unit was primarily a work farm, and staff members placed new prisoners in the fields to work. Due to reductions in staffing levels and new security mandates, the prison's agricultural operations were curtailed.[10] In 2008 the Texas Board of Criminal Justice unanimously voted to rename the Gatesville Unit after Christina Melton Crain, the first female chairperson of the Texas Board of Criminal Justice; on that day the name change was effective immediately.[2] Crain, a Dallas lawyer, left the Texas Board of Criminal Justice in May 2008.[11]

Location, composition, and operations

Aerial photograph of the prisons in Gatesville, January 13, 1996, <u>United States Geological Survey</u>

The Christina Crain Unit houses all non-death row custody levels and is equipped to hold 2,014 prisoners. Crain consists of several separate satellite units, each serving a distinct purpose.[12]

Crain's Reception Center is the place where new female arrivals to the TDCJ are processed. In addition the center houses a <u>boot camp</u> program.[13] The 174 bed Valley Unit houses pregnant, elderly, and mentally retarded prisoners.[13] As of 1993 72 beds are reserved for the mentally retarded.[12] In addition Valley houses the prison library.[13] Female prisoners throughout Texas who are not state jail prisoners or substance abuse felony punishment facility residents are released from the Crain Unit.[14]

Most women in Crain live in dormitories described by Leah Karotkin of the _Houston Press_ as "drab" and "low-slung." Most inmates work seven hours per day. Jobs include painting and repairing buildings, maintaining and repairing large equipment such as boiler units, hoeing fields, and fixing potholes.[15] Crain includes a trustee camp, which was one of the first to be built by the TDCJ. The camp, which has no perimeter fence, houses non-violent minimum custody inmates who need less supervision than regular inmates and who are less likely to escape than regular inmates. The trustees live in an open dormitory and work in prisoner and prison guard beauty shops, food service, landscaping, and transportation.[15] Women in the Valley Unit work as beauty operators, clerks, cooks, kitchen workers, and landscape gardeners. Women who cannot work in those jobs work in the Special Projects Program by making crafts; they are permitted to sell their crafts for commisary money, and church groups and prison guards are some of the customers.[13] Crain has 20 beds available for the Sentence

Alternative to Incarceration Program, a 90 day program for first time offenders between the ages of 17 and 25. The boot camp is housed in a former infirmary in the Reception Center. 32 isolation cells are reserved for difficult prisoners.[13]

As of 1993 women who are about to give birth are transported to the Hospital Galveston unit in Galveston, which is located five hours away from Gatesville by automobile.[16]

Prisoner life

In 1993 Leah Karotkin of the *Houston Press* said "Anticipating my visit to Gatesville, I had expected more drama. Instead, I was struck by the simple endless monotony of the prison, disappointingly mundane rather than what I expected. More than hard-time punishment, alienation and loneliness seem to be the goals, or at least the most obvious effects, of the institution. Still, it's clear, Gatesville is a pretty rough place to be."[17] In 2010 Robert Perkinson, author of *Texas Tough: The Rise of America's Prison Empire*, said that Crain was "not the hardest place to do time in Texas."[18]

Major Janice Wilson, who was the head prison guard in 1993, said during that year that many women in Crain gain close bonds with women who they sympathize or feel sorry for. Some women had been in romantic relationships where they received battery, and some had experienced several romantic relationships that, to them, were not good. According to Wilson these women become friends, and some of the women engage in homosexual relationships. As of 1993 the institution forbids sexual conduct between two prisoners, and women can lose class time if they are caught.[15] In several published reports that existed by 1993, prisoners said that the isolation is a factor in the sexual relationships that are formed at the unit. Wilson added that the aspect many women dislike the most about Crain is the lack of accessibility to their families and children. For many, visits occur infrequently and women do not often get to make telephone calls. Many relatives have very little money and do not have much time that they can use to visit their imprisoned relatives.

Wilson said that a constant underlying internal tension existed at Crain.[13]

Programs

Robert Perkinson, author of *Texas Tough: The Rise of America's Prison Empire*, said that the Crain Unit has a "rich assortment of programming" compared to most Texas prisons. The unit includes a female boot camp and a Substance Abuse Felony Punishment (SAFP) facility.[19]

• .

.

About The Author

Robert writes True Crime books am a first-generation American of Argentine Italian and German descent. I like to write about real life I follow and write about criminal trials and serial killers and their victims. We must never forget that they are victims are real people. That genre I write about is called true crime . My book Gone With The Night followed the case of Dennis Dalton after the murders of Gracie and Tiffany. My second book, red notice.

I follow the murder trial of Jessica Tata and what happened to her victims in a local Houston daycare fire. The children ranged in age from 36 months to six months. My book uncovered that she had two prior convictions for arson fires . One in her high school cafeteria at Dolby high school and one in the girls bathroom. The state of Texas never did a proper or complete background check on her before issuing a license to her. It turns out that the agency that was regulating her daycare is also regulating her in prison same social services caseworkers will be looking in on her as well. I took this personally because I'm dependent on help as well. I have a disability for birth cerebral palsy that requires me to use a motorized wheelchair and have additional assistance in the form of attendant care and therapy services, without which I could not live a productive life. And I am very thankful for, but I also know that I'm at the mercy of those that care or do not care if I wrote these books. It was not for the money it for. It was more for the peace and healing, because both of these situations were tragic and unforeseen by the people in charge. I hope that none of this is ever forgotten Robert

www.ingramcontent.com/pod-product-compliance
Lightning Source LLC
Chambersburg PA
CBHW070303290526
45791CB00003B/1072